THE ARABS KNEW

Also by Tillie S. Pine and Joseph Levine

with pictures by Ann Grifalconi

THE AFRICANS KNEW
THE INCAS KNEW
THE MAYA KNEW

with pictures by Marilyn Hirsh

THE POLYNESIANS KNEW

with pictures by Ezra Jack Keats

THE CHINESE KNEW
THE EGYPTIANS KNEW
THE ESKIMOS KNEW
THE INDIANS KNEW
THE PILGRIMS KNEW

with pictures by Bernice Myers

AIR ALL AROUND
ELECTRICITY AND HOW WE USE IT
FRICTION ALL AROUND
GRAVITY ALL AROUND
HEAT ALL AROUND
LIGHT ALL AROUND
ROCKS AND HOW WE USE THEM
SIMPLE MACHINES AND HOW WE USE THEM
SOUNDS ALL AROUND
TREES AND HOW WE USE THEM
WATER ALL AROUND
WEATHER ALL AROUND

with pictures by Anne Marie Jauss

MAGNETS AND HOW WE USE THEM

with pictures by Harriet Sherman

MEASUREMENTS AND HOW WE USE THEM

with pictures by Joel Schick

ENERGY ALL AROUND

The ARABS Knew

by **TILLIE S. PINE** and **JOSEPH LEVINE**
illustrated by **JOEL SCHICK**

McGRAW-HILL BOOK COMPANY

NEW YORK   ST. LOUIS   SAN FRANCISCO   AUCKLAND   DÜSSELDORF
JOHANNESBURG   KUALA LUMPUR   LONDON   MEXICO
MONTREAL   NEW DELHI   PANAMA   PARIS
SAO PAULO   SINGAPORE   SYDNEY
TOKYO   TORONTO

To the memory of Herman,

*whose appreciation of other cultures
sparked his devotion to peace among nations.*

LIBRARY OF CONGRESS CATALOGING IN PUBLICATION DATA

Pine, Tillie S
  The Arabs knew.

  1. Arabs—Juvenile literature. 2. Technology
—Juvenile literature. I. Levine, Joseph,
1910-   joint author. II. Schick, Joel.
III. Title.
DS36.78.P56   909'.04'927   76-17824
ISBN 0-07-050091-6 lib. bdg.

123456 RABP 789876

About The Book

The Arabs Knew tells you about the two kinds of Arabs who lived in Arabia many hundreds of years ago. There were the Arabs who lived in the hot, dry desert and were called *Bedouins*. The other Arabs lived in cities near and far away from the desert.

The desert Arabs were nomads. They moved from watering place to watering place with their camel and sheep caravans. They knew and did many things that helped them survive in their fierce surroundings. They knew how to protect themselves against the desert climate. They knew how to use the camel to make their life and their work easier. They even knew how to keep their drinking water cool without ice!

Some of the leading city Arabs became very much interested in science, medicine, mathematics, education, and other learnings. They studied the great books that were written by Greek, Persian, Hebrew, and Hindu scholars thousands of years before them, and they rewrote many of these books into the Arabic language. The Arab scientists and physicians invented new methods of working in science and mathematics— methods which we still use today.

The Arabs soon conquered many countries and many Arabs settled down in these conquered lands. They built schools and libraries and set about educating the people who lived there.

The Arabs Knew describes what the desert Arabs and the city Arabs knew and did long ago. It also tells you what you can do to increase your understanding of these people.

The Arabs Knew

how to make use of the camel to help them live in the desert. The camel is a strong animal. It can carry a load weighing up to 500 pounds and can travel many days without water. It has long, double eyelashes which protect its eyes against blowing sand and large, fleshy foot pads which keep its feet from sinking into the sand. The desert Arabs used the camel to carry them and their goods across the hot desert. They drank the camel's milk and ate its meat. They used the camel hides for their tents and for covers. The Bedouins also used dried camel dung as fuel for their fires.

They called the camel *Ata Allah*—God's Gift. Without the camel, these Arabs could not have survived in the desert.

Today

many other desert people still use the camel in their daily living, just as the Bedouins still do. Some desert people also use jeeps, cars, and even airplanes to travel across the desert. Many people in different countries use the camel's hair to make clothing and fine paint brushes for artists.

You

can visit the zoo and see the one-humped camel that the desert Arabs use. It is called the *Dromedary* camel. You can also see the two-humped camel that the desert people in Asia use. It is called the *Bactrian* camel.

The Arabs Knew

where they could find water in the hot, dry desert. They knew that certain parts of the desert had large valleys, or gullies, which they called *wadis*. Rainstorms did not come very often, but the desert Arabs knew that when the rains did come, the wadis would fill up with water. After a while, the wadis would dry up until the next sudden rainstorm.

They also knew that in certain parts of their huge desert, there were underground streams that flowed from distant hills. The desert Arabs built wells so that they could bring up water from these underground streams. Grass and date-palm trees grew at these watering places. We call these green places *oases*.

When the desert Arabs traveled in their camel-caravans across the desert to trade their goods and animals, they followed the routes that led from watering place to watering place.

Today

the desert Arabs in their camel-caravans still follow the same routes that led them from oasis to oasis in the Arabian desert. In the southwestern part of the United States, there is desert land in which we find large gullies. We call these gullies *arroyos.* Sudden rainstorms fill up these arroyos, which hold water and then also dry up until the next sudden rainstorm.

You

can do something that will help you understand how rainwater can fill small valleys or gullies.

Put about four inches of sand into a wide box outdoors. Roll out a piece of play-clay thin and flat. Lay it on the sand and push in the center of the clay to make it look like a saucer. This is your "gulley" in your "desert."

Fill a toy watering can with water and sprinkle the water over your desert. See how the water sinks into the sand while the gully fills up and holds the rainwater.

You can also see how rainfall fills small gullies in soil. Walk in the park or in a field and look for gullies. After a rainfall, see how these gullies hold water as the ground around them dries up.

The Arabs Knew

how to build shelters to protect themselves against
the desert climate.

The desert Arabs made tents out of camel hides. They
set up these tents when they stopped traveling over the
desert and then took them down when they continued
on their journey.

The poor Arabs in the villages made one-room houses
out of sun-dried mud with flat roofs and bare dirt floors.
Each roof had a small hole in it through which the smoke
of their cooking fire could escape. They kept their
animals in a stall next to the one-room house.

The wealthy city Arabs built their houses of mud bricks
or stone blocks around courtyards paved with marble
tiles. Their houses had pointed, arched roofs which
were held up by stone columns. The many rooms of
these houses were beautifully decorated with
ornaments and rugs.

Today

people all over the world live in houses of all kinds, but many people still use tents for shelter. Most of these tents are made in factories out of different rainproof materials. Tents are used by campers and hunters, and in circuses and fairs. In many parts of the world, some people live in tents all year, just as the Bedouins still do.

You

can make a model of a desert scene.
Use a large, shallow cardboard box. Cover the bottom of the box with sand. Make an Arab tent out of small twigs and cloth. Make an oasis, using pipe cleaners and green construction paper for palm trees. Make stick figures of Bedouin families and their camels.

The Arabs Knew

that white clothing would keep them cool in the hot desert climate, so they wore long white robes to cover their bodies and white cloths tied with camel's hair to cover their heads. They knew that, in this way, they could keep most of the heat of the sun's rays from going through their clothing and making them hot and uncomfortable.

Today

we often wear light-colored clothing to keep us cool in hot weather. We know that light colors keep most of the sun's rays from getting through our clothing to our bodies. We say light colors *reflect* the sun's rays. We also paint gas and oil tanks white to keep the gas and oil inside the tanks from getting too hot. Many people who live in warm climates have light-colored roofs put on their houses to reflect the sun's rays. This keeps the houses cooler.

You

can prove that light colors reflect the sun's rays. You need two house thermometers of the same kind and size, a piece of white cloth, and a piece of dark cloth. Put both thermometers in the shade outdoors. After five minutes, read the temperatures of both thermometers. Write down the temperature of each. Now, cover one thermometer with the white cloth, the other with the dark cloth, and place both in the sunshine. After ten minutes, take the thermometers into the shade, uncover them, and read the temperatures immediately. Which thermometer shows a lower temperature? Why?

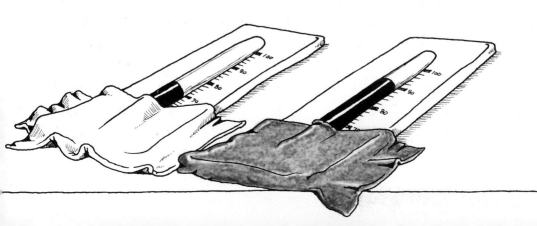

The Arabs Knew

how to keep drinking water cool and fresh when they
traveled through the hot desert.

The desert Arabs made bags out of goatskin and filled
them with water. They knew that a very small amount
of the water would slowly seep through to the outside
surface of the goatskin bag. This surface water
evaporated into the air under the hot sun. As the water
evaporated from the surface of the goatskin water bag,
the evaporation cooled the bag and the water inside the
bag. This kept the water cool and fresh.

Today

we know that evaporation can cool. Our bodies perspire. As the perspiration evaporates into the air, the evaporation cools our skin. This makes us feel cooler and more comfortable in hot weather. Nurses in hospitals give their patients alcohol rubs. They know that the alcohol on the skin evaporates quickly into the air—even more quickly than water evaporates. This makes the patient feel cooler and more comfortable.

You

can prove that evaporation cools things.

Put some cool water into a bowl and let it stand on a table for about fifteen minutes. This will bring the water to the same temperature as the air in the room. Put two wall thermometers of the same kind and size on the table. After a few minutes, write down the temperature shown on each thermometer. The two temperatures should be the same. Dip a handkerchief into the water, wring it out, spread it out, and wrap it around the bulb of one thermometer. Wrap a dry handkerchief around the bulb of the other thermometer. After ten minutes, read the temperature again on each thermometer. Are the two temperatures the same? The temperature of the thermometer wrapped in the wet handkerchief is lower because, as the water in the handkerchief evaporated into the air, it cooled the thermometer and the temperature went down.

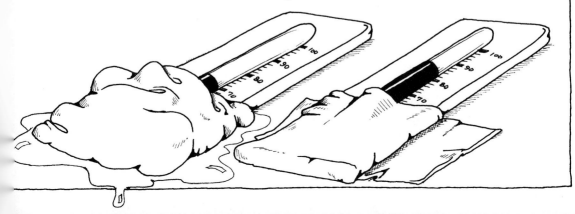

The Arabs Knew

how to conduct scientific experiments. The city Arabs
invented the steps by which to conduct them.
When they wanted to find the answer to a problem in
science, they selected the materials they needed; they
experimented with these materials; they observed
carefully what was happening; they wrote down exactly
what they saw; and, from what they saw happening,
they found the answer to the problem.
Arab scientists carried out many chemistry experiments
in this way.

Today

our scientists use the same method when they conduct experiments in chemistry, biology, physics, and even in the science of space. We call this way of working the *scientific method.*

You

can solve a science problem by using the scientific method.

What happens when water is exposed to the air? You need two plastic containers and some water.

Put the two containers on the windowsill side by side. Pour the same amount of water into each container. Mark the level of the water with tape or crayon. Cover one container. After five days, take the cover off this container. Which container has less water? The one that was not covered has. Why?

Some of the water in the uncovered container evaporated into the air. The water in the covered container was not exposed to the air and, therefore, did not evaporate.

Do you understand why some people hang wet clothes outdoors on a line?

The Arabs Knew

how light really helps people see things.
Up to 1,000 years ago, scientists all over the world
believed that people see things because the light rays
come from the eyes and shine on the things that they
look at. The Arab scientist, al-Hazen, discovered that
this was not so. He found out and explained that people
see things because light from the sun and from burning
things shine on these things, and these things send back,
or *reflect,* that light to the eyes. He, therefore, showed
that reflected light makes it possible for the eyes to
see things.

Today

we know that reflected light makes it possible for us to see things. Of course, we have the light of the sun, the moon, and burning things to help us, just as it helped the people of long ago, but today we also have electricity to give us light of many kinds.

So—we have all kinds of light, natural and artificial, that shine on things and make it possible for us to see these things by reflected light.

You

can find out for yourself that we see things because things reflect the light that hits them.

Go into a closet. Close the door. What do you see? Nothing! Why?

Now open the door slightly. Can you see anything in the closet at this time? Why? When you open the door, you let light into the closet.

The light shines on things in the closet, these things reflect the light to your eyes, and—you see them.

The Arabs Knew

that we see things in *perspective*. This means that when something is far away from the eye, it seems small. When it is closer to the eye, it seems larger.
The Arab scientist, al-Hazen, discovered why this is so about 1,000 years ago.

He knew that light rays move in straight lines. He found out that when these rays come through the lens of the eye, they bend. These bent rays meet and form an image on the back of the eye. When he looked at a tree that was far away from him, it looked small because the image in his eye was small. When he looked at a tree that was closer to him, it looked larger because the image in his eye was larger.

Today

we, too, know we see things in perspective.
Artists make use of perspective when they draw or
paint things as they see them. When an artist paints
a tree in the background of his picture, he paints it
small to show that it is far away. When he paints a tree
in the foreground of his picture, he paints it large to
show that it is near.

You

can do something to help you understand how things
seem to change size in perspective.
Stand five steps away from a picture on your wall.
Look at the picture. Hold a pencil by one end straight
up at arm's length. Close one eye. Make sure that the
top end of the pencil is even with the top of the picture.
Now, move your thumb down the pencil until it seems
to touch the bottom of the picture. Make a mark on the
pencil where your thumbnail is. Now, move five steps
farther back and do the same thing. Are the marks
on the pencil in the same place?
Do you understand how seeing in perspective makes
the same picture seem smaller or larger depending upon
how far you are standing from it?

The Arabs Knew

how to set up a real drugstore or *pharmacy* (far-masee)
in their cities. They were the first people to do this.
They were also the first people to set up a school to
teach students to become pharmacists. The students
had to pass examinations in order to get certificates.
With these certificates, the Arab pharmacists could
open drugstores where they could make and sell all
kinds of medicines.

The Arab scientists were the first ones to keep written
lists of the 760 different kinds of drugs and medicines
they knew about and used.

Today

our druggists fill doctors' prescriptions in drugstores where many other things are sold. However, we still have apothecary shops where only prescriptions and medicines are sold.

Our pharmacists are also trained in colleges and must pass examinations to get their licenses to fill doctors' prescriptions.

You

can visit a drugstore and ask the pharmacist to show you how he fills doctors' prescriptions and what records he has to keep.

You might also ask him to show you the thick book which lists all the different kinds of medicines we have today. See if you can find the pharmacist's license hanging on the wall.

The Arabs Knew

how to make up a number system that was easy to use.
Before numerals were used, people wrote numbers out
in words or letters. Some people, like the Chinese,
used the abacus in working with numbers.
The Arabs changed the Hindu numerals one through
nine into Arabic numerals.

These early Arabic numerals looked like this:

9 8 7 6 5 4 3 2 1

An Arab mathematician also invented the zero and
added the symbol "0" (for zero) to the written number
system we still use today.
The Arabic word for zero is *sifr,* which means "empty."
The Arabic number system changed the whole way of
working with numbers. It made addition, subtraction,
multiplication, and division easier to work with. We still
call the numerals 0 through 9 *Arabic* numerals.

Today

we use Arabic numerals when we do examples in writing or "in our heads." Sometimes, we use calculators to help us. We also have invented computers to help us solve many difficult number problems.

You

can find out how important the zero is when you work with numbers.

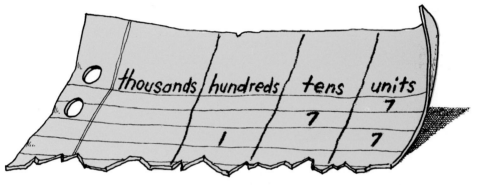

Make four columns. Label the columns, from right to left, "units," "tens," "hundreds," "thousands." The picture shows you how. Write the number seven in the correct column. Now, without using the zero, write the number seventy, one hundred seven and one thousand seven in the correct columns, one number under the other. On another paper, write these numbers one under the other, but this time use the zero when you need to. Do you see how easy it is to write numbers when you use the zero? The zero is really a place holder in our number work.

Can you write the answers to these examples without using the zero?

$$16 + 4 \quad =$$
$$204 - 103 =$$
$$8 \times 5 \quad =$$
$$20 \div 2 \quad =$$

The Arabs Knew

that the earth was round and not flat, as almost all
people believed over 1,000 years ago.

The city Arabs learned this by reading ancient Greek
and Hindu writings, and, when they traveled, the Arabs
taught this to other people in many countries.

Christopher Columbus read about this in Spanish-Arab
science books 400 years later. He believed so much that
the earth was not flat that he sailed westward from
Spain to find a new route to the East. He did not find
the new route, but he did find a new world.

Today

our scientists study the earth very carefully. They use special instruments to measure the roundness and the size of the earth accurately. Our astronauts and our unmanned space ships take pictures of our earth from far off in space. They even send back television pictures to us on earth that show that the earth is like a great round ball.

You

can see that the planet Earth is round.

If you live near the ocean, look across the water and note where the water and the sky appear to meet. We call this point the *horizon.* See if you can spot a ship sailing toward the horizon. As the ship sails farther and farther away from you, does it seem to sink lower and lower into the ocean? Does it finally disappear? Why? Do this. It will help you understand.

Hold a large ball straight out in the palm of your hand. Hold a pencil in your other hand, and slowly move the pencil over the top of the ball from front to back. The pencil disappears because it follows the curve of the ball until the ball hides the pencil.

In the same way, the ship follows the curve of the earth until the earth hides the ship. The ship disappears.

The Arabs Knew

what causes the ocean tides. An Arab scientist discovered the cause over 1,000 years ago.

He knew that the moon slowly moves around the earth as the earth turns. He found out that the moon, the sun, and the earth pull on each other. We call this pull the *gravitational pull.* No one can see this pull, but it is there. The Arab scientist discovered that this pull causes the ocean waters to get higher and lower. The rising and the falling of the water are the ocean tides. He also knew that there are two high tides and two low tides each day.

Today

it is very important for many people to know about the high tides and low tides.

Builders of docks must know about the heights of different tides when they build the docks so that their docks will always be above water.

Captains and pilots of large ships must know about tides so that they can safely steer their ships in and out of ports at high tide.

People who build houses along the ocean shores must also know about tides so that the ocean water cannot reach their houses at the highest tides.

You

can find out the times when high tides and low tides happen every day.

Most of the newspapers print this information under "Weather Reports" or under "Shipping News." If you live near the ocean shore, you can see how high the the water reaches on the beach during high tide and how low it is during low tide. You can also find the water marks on beams and on pier posts in the water.

The Arabs Knew

how to spread their learning to people in other parts of the world.

They probably were the first people to do so, and they did it without newspapers, telephones, radio, or television.

They wrote many books. They also rewrote, into their Arabic language, the books of great authors who had written in other languages, such as Greek, Hindu, Persian, and Hebrew. Wherever they went to live, they set up schools, colleges, and libraries. In these ways, they spread their knowledge and their language to the people all around them.

Today

we use many different ways to spread learning. We build schools, colleges, and universities—each with its own library. We train teachers, who use all kinds of audio-visual aids to help them teach. We print books, magazines, and newspapers in many languages. We make use of radio, television, microfilm, and all kinds of learning machines.

You

can teach others what you have learned.
If there is a foreign-speaking child in your class or in your neighborhood, you can help that child to learn your language. You can show your friends how to play a game you know, how to sing a new song you learned, how to sew or knit, or even how to do a science experiment.

You can also show your friends how to write the early Arabic numerals that you found in this book. You can even teach your friends how to write the title of this book in Arabic:

$$\text{"ما يعرفه العربى"}$$

(ma yarifoho al-Arabi)

You write and read Arabic from right to left. The title in Arabic means *What the Arabs Knew*. So, you see— you, too, can spread learning all around.

The Arab scientists of the cities had a great deal of knowledge that helped people all over the world. The city Arabs of long ago knew and did many things that help scientists today.

Arab astronomers made better instruments to help sailors find their way across the ocean. They measured the size of the earth very accurately. They studied the stars and the planets, and they made an almost perfect calendar.

Some of the most important things in science were done by great Arab doctors like al-Razi and ibn-Sina. They:

- recognized many diseases like smallpox and measles and understood the importance of quarantine.
- discovered 130 different eye diseases and were able to cure many of them.
- knew how to operate on people to help cure serious illnesses (Abu-al-Qasim was the greatest of the Arab surgeons).
- built medical schools and hospitals.
- wrote many medical books.
- set up traveling clinics to reach and treat people who were far away.
- explained the importance of good diet and personal hygiene.
- even trained veterinarians to treat sick animals.

Now that you have read *The Arabs Knew,* don't you agree that the Arabs really had many different science understandings so long, long ago?